Countryside Houses Coloring Book For Adults

Collection of 50 Pastoral Village Landscape Sketches

Rachel Mintz

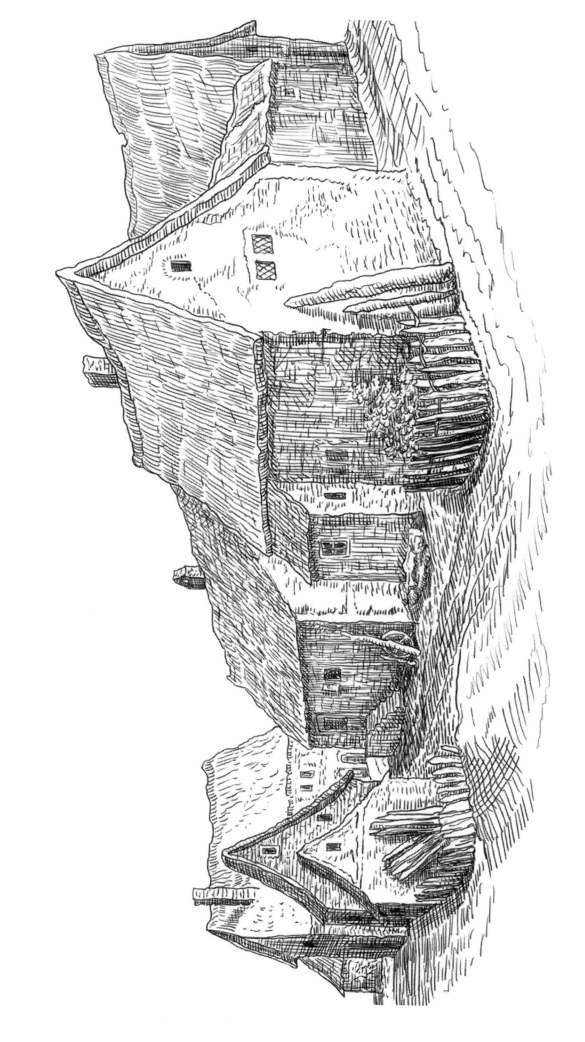

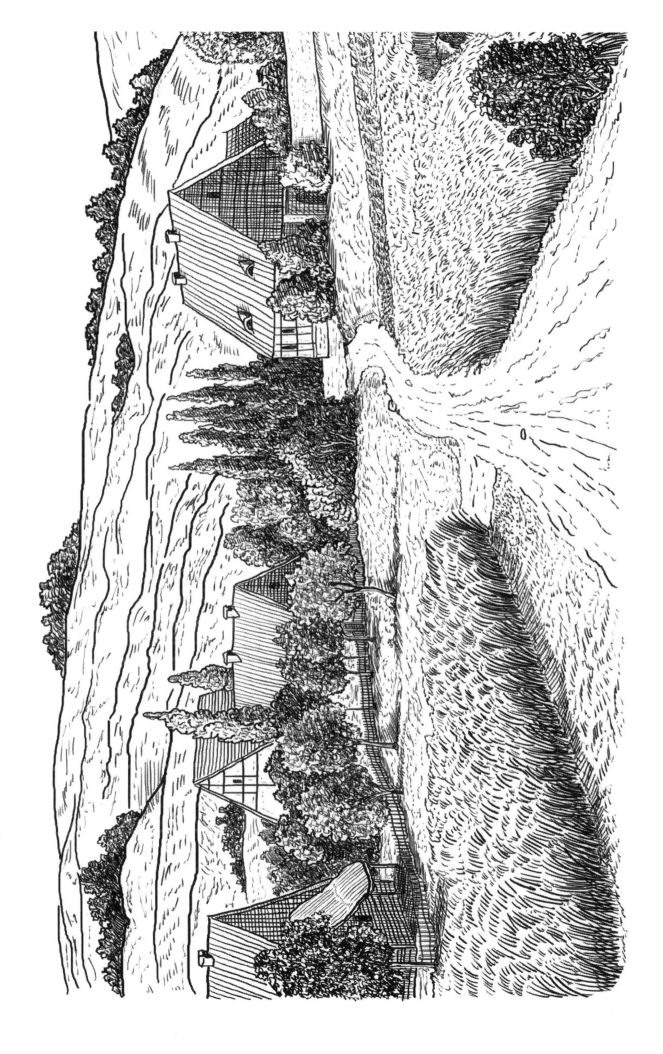

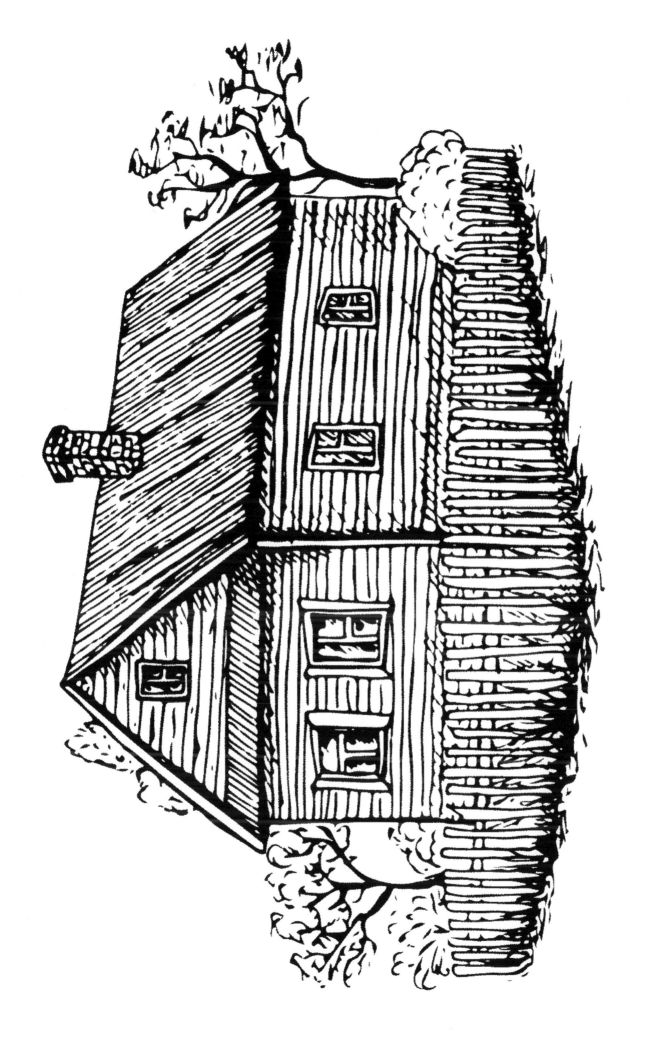

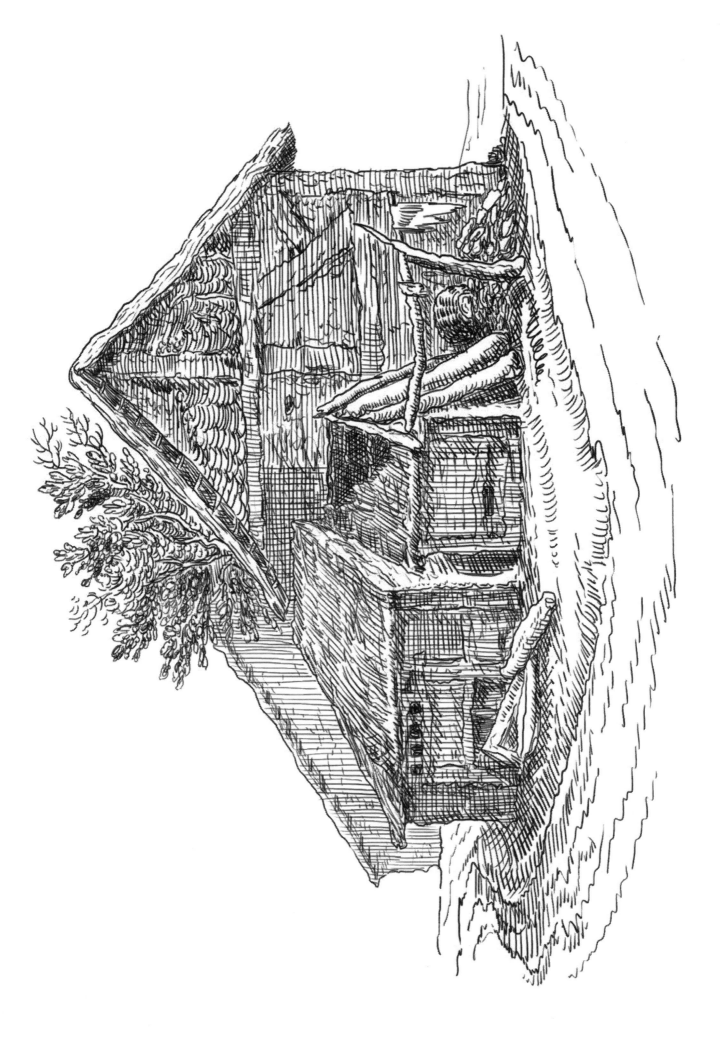

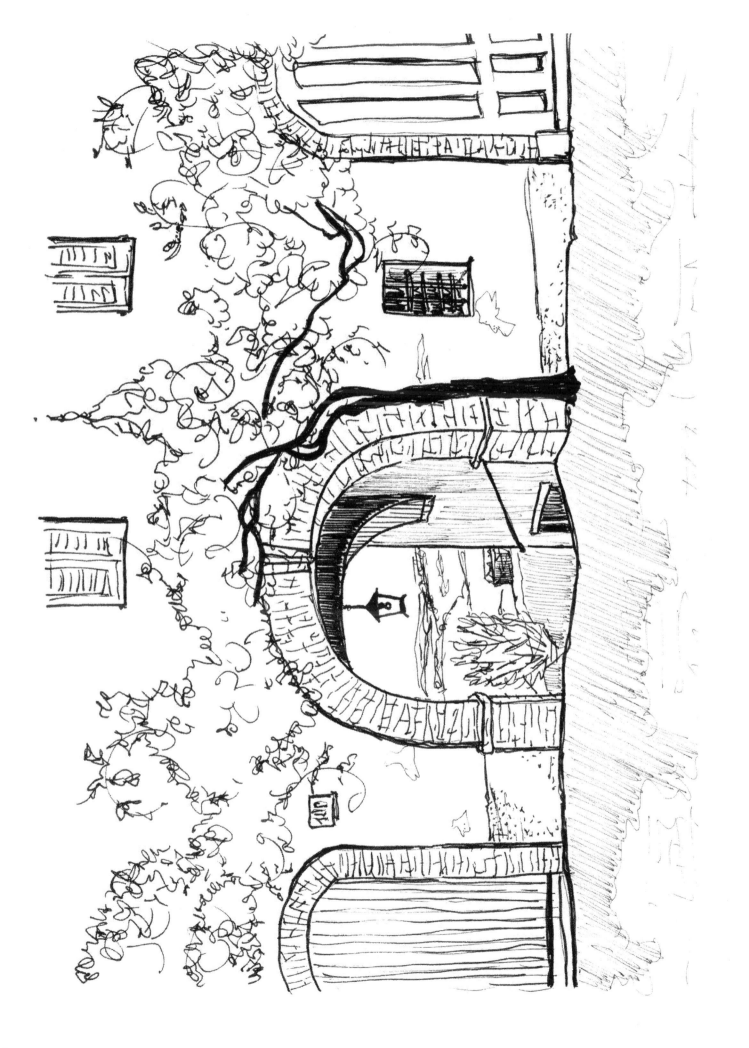

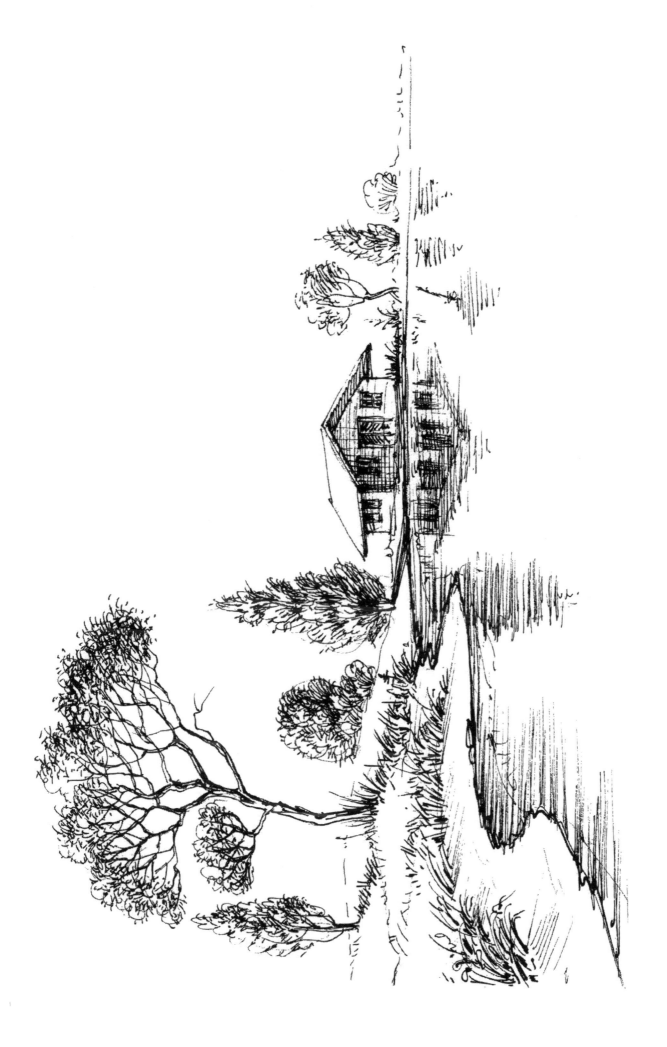

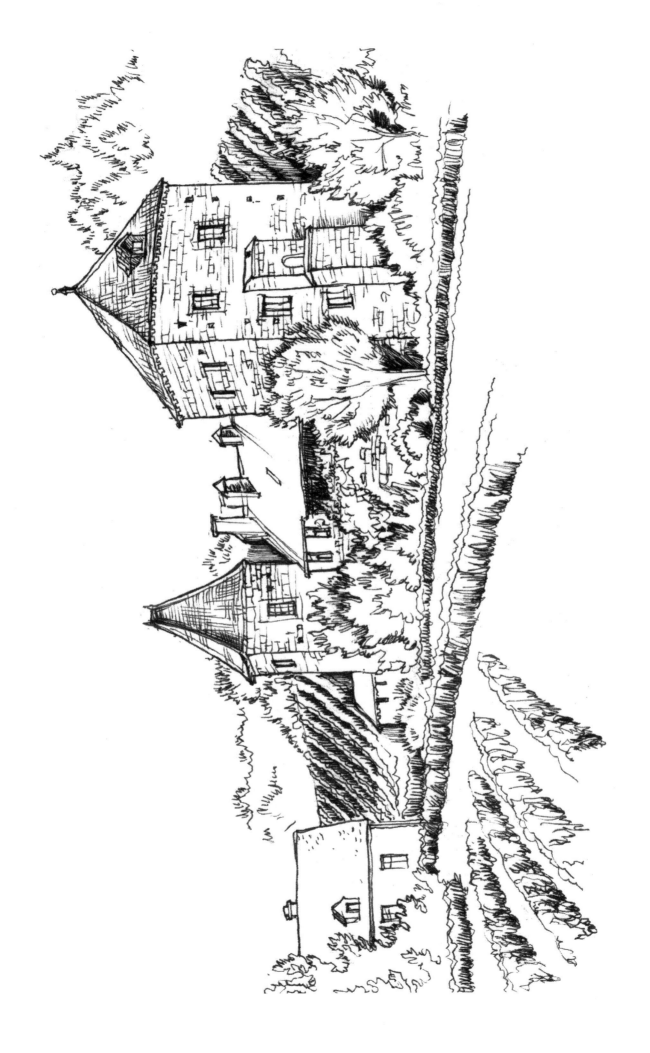

Thank you for coloring with us
Please consider to rate & review

More from our coloring books:

BEAUTIFUL LIGHTHOUSES
COLORING BOOK

RACHEL MINTZ

Venice
Moments

Rachel Mintz   Coloring Book

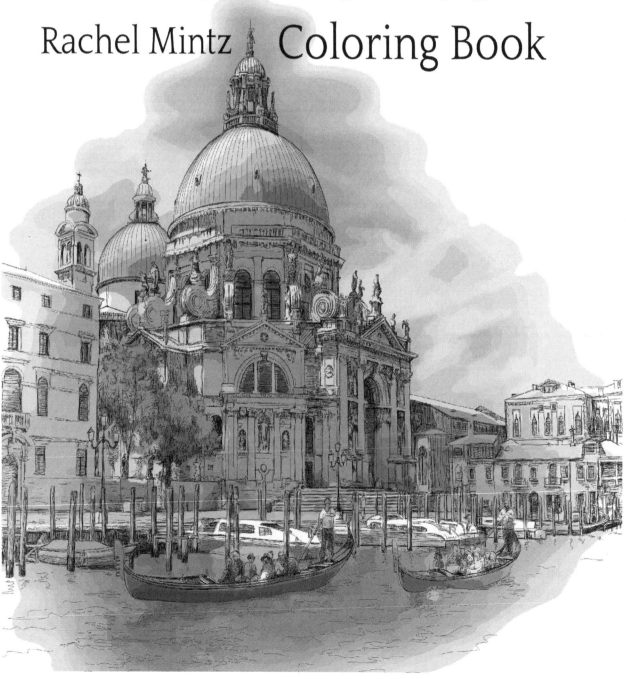

Thank you for coloring with us

Made in the USA
Middletown, DE
18 July 2018